The Dad Joke Bible

The Dad Joke Bible

Plastician selects the best worst jokes ever.

CHRIS REED

DISCLAIMER

This book is a selection of my favorite jokes. Many of which are my own jokes, or jokes inspired by jokes I've heard or discovered online. There are also a lot of the best jokes I've seen on the internet or been told by people. As is the case with jokes which are told and shared the world over, whether by word of mouth, or posting on the web, crediting and verifying the originators of said jokes can be difficult. I've made efforts not to use any jokes that can be credited to their original performer from a verified source via research. If you believe you are the original writer of any of the jokes within the pages of this book, and are not credited as such, or wish to be removed from the pages please email stishcast@gmail.com with proof.

INTRO

My name is Chris Reed, many people already know me as Plastician, a South London based DJ and producer. I've built a career for myself that spans 2 decades traversing the highs and lows of the music industry starting out as a telesales person for a distribution company, and peaking as a global touring artist who played music in every continent on the globe barring antarctica before the age of 25.

For years people have been telling me I should write a book. I thought that sounded like a great idea for a time when I have some decent stories or knowledge to share. Fast forward a few years and here I am, my first book. And the knowledge I am about to share? Well I don't think it's the same kind of knowledge my peers expected of me but it's certainly some things I think many of you will make good use of in your day to day existence. In fact, at the end of the year 2020 it is probably likely that this book will be pretty useful to help lift the clouds of dread that hang over your masked head. I hope it raises a smile for you and the people you share this with, we all need a laugh occasionally.

So here it is. A collection of some of the best "Dad" jokes you'll find anywhere. Tweets from the archives, unearthed gems from the depths of the internet, and straight fire off the top of the dome. Delivered to you via the pages of my first ever publication. If this sells well I might even consider writing about music one day, but no promises are being made yet.

ACKNOWLEDGMENTS

This book is for my wife Caroline. She puts up with me hiding away in the garage most days and now she knows what I'm doing in here. I love you dearly. I must also shout out my Mum & Dad, who've brought me up and are responsible for this sense of humor (well, Dad probably is). John my brother who will also appreciate the levels of banter in here – hope you, Kim and Harley (one day) enjoy it! My kids Jackson & Eden will probably have to wait a few more years to understand how funny their Dad is, but I could not print these pages without letting them know their Dad loves them both dearly and this book goes to show you both that you can do anything you want to in this world... Just google how to do it first. Special mentions to all the Moore side! Nick, Bridget, Hayley, Neil, Steve, Melissa, Nicky, Lucy, Cesca – and big hugs to Jacob, Georgina and Talia as well!

Dedicated to Nobby Moore. He loved a bad joke as much as I do. We miss you brother! X

Why is the Apple Store so hot?

Because they don't install Windows.

This is the worst spell of wether I've seen in a while.

Why are gold diggers such private people?

They mined their own business.

My friend had to leave his job at the gym because he was not strong enough.

He's just handed in his too weak notice.

What did the Koala pack for his weekend away?

Just the bear essentials.

Sir Alex Ferguson's race horses.

They're a knight mare to look after.

Started following Vin Diesel on Instagram.

He's a tough actor follow.

Got one of those beer deliveries during lockdown and they just threw the cans on my roof.

They said the first month's delivery is on the house.

How do you make Holy Water?

Boil the hell out of it.

What do you think Elton John's favourite lettuce is?

I think he's a bit of a rocket man.

Did I tell you about the guy who dipped his testicles in glitter?

Pretty nuts.

What's made of leather and sounds like a sneeze?

A shoe.

The flag is not the main reason to move to Switzerland.

But it is a big plus.

Saturday and Sunday are the strongest days of the week.

All the others are weak days.

My Dog will not stop chewing our new sofa.

He's got a suite tooth.

My wife is a nurse at the local urologist.

She takes the piss.

Did you know Cardi-B used to be a fitness instructor?

She used to be called Cardi-O.

I don't trust stairs.

They're always up to something.

I didn't like beards

But then they grew on me.

Have you heard the story about the three wells?

Well, well, well.

I asked a guy in the headphone store "what's the best for noise cancellation"?

He said I should try Pioneers.

Chicken & Mushroom was useless but I'm trying Steak & Ale tonight.

People say I have no will power.

But I've quit smoking loads of times.

I overdosed on Viagra once.

Hardest day of my life.

The UK is so upset with the COVID-19 measures.

The whole country is in tiers.

Got a PS5 for my kids this Christmas.

Best trade I ever made.

Don't tell jokes about retired people.

None of them work.

With great power...

Comes great electricity bill.

I feel really sorry for the class of 2020. People say your final year at University flies.

Nobody realized it would Zoom.

It's inappropriate to make a Dad joke if you're not a Dad.

It's a faux Pa.

Why can't your tongue be 12 inches long?

Because then it would be a foot.

Tips for finding Will Smith in a snowstorm?

Look out for the fresh prints.

As I get older and remember all the people I've lost down the years...

I realize a career as a tour guide wasn't for me.

I'm annoyed with my room mate for losing one of my Mr Men books.

No more "Mr Nice Guy".

A woman asked if I had any good jokes about euphemisms.

So I gave her one.

Did you hear about the man who fell into the well?

He didn't see that well.

Classroom whiteboards are a remarkable invention.

A broken drumkit is the best Christmas present.

You can't beat it.

What is blue and doesn't weigh very much?

Light blue.

Be careful around French people.

They eat pain for breakfast.

My friends at school thought my interest in cows was weird.

They just couldn't accept that I had udder interests.

Why do hipsters always burn their hands on the frying pan?

They pick it up before it's cool.

I don't really get why I have such a dislike for scarves.

Just can't wrap my head around them.

Why did the baker have dirty hands?

He kneaded a poo.

Buying flowers for somebody is a kind surprise.

But chocolate eggs are a Kinder Surprise.

Had a bad accident last week falling into an upholstery machine.

I'm fully recovered now though.

Did anyone see the joke I posted about the chiropractor?

It was about a weak back?

There's a guy stealing iPhones in my area.

He's probably going to facetime.

Lost my keys this morning. My wife told me to look harder.

So I shaved my head and got a tattoo. Still can't find my keys.

Couldn't figure out how to fix my mouse this morning.

But then it just clicked.

My stoner friend is a great bartender.

He sets the bar very high.

You can't use BEEFSTEW as a password.

It's not Stroganoff.

Had a pelican curry last night.

Tasted great! Massive bill though.

Got an email about reading maps backwards.

Turns out it's spam.

Asked the chemist what is best for killing germs.

"Ammonia Cleaner" they said back.

I said "sorry, I thought you worked here".

My dad's job raises a few eyebrows.

He's a plastic surgeon.

I didn't hear my wife warning me I was holding the pasta bag upside down.

But then the penne dropped.

I've stopped eating venison and moved onto grouse instead.

It's a game changer.

My Grandad told me to take everything in life with a pinch of salt.

Great man, made a horrible cup of tea though.

Found my first grey hair today.

Unfortunately it was in my Big Mac.

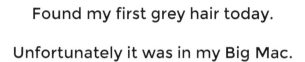

My friend sprayed deodorant into his mouth.

He now speaks with a strong Axe scent.

Went to the zoo yesterday and there was a ciabatta in a cage.

It was bread in captivity.

I used to DJ at Stonehenge.

I don't mix in that circle anymore though.

What's the oldest age you can get a circumcision?

Just wondered what the cut-off date was.

What did Yoda say when he saw himself in 4K?

HDMI?

Putting in contact lenses for the first time was a real eye opener.

I asked the lady in the bookstore if they had any books on Turtles..
Hardback? She asked.

"Yes, and with little heads" I said.

Been hard to share my jokes during lockdown.

Most of them are inside jokes.

My Wife said I'm always overthinking stuff.

I can't figure out what she means by that.

John Travolta thought he'd contracted Coronavirus over the weekend.

Turns out it was just a Saturday Night Fever though.

The best music producers suffer badly with piles.

They're always sat on heaters.

Shoutout to whoever invented the number 0.

Thanks for nothing.

Had a DJ set in Mumbai last night.

A Bombay Mix if you will.

15 years after Friends ended and people are still making references to it.

No one told me life was gonna be this way.

Just seen a broken iPod advertised. Free to pick up but the volume is stuck on full.

I thought there's no way I can turn that down.

Nothing tops a plain pizza.

What do you call a chameleon who can't change colour?

A reptile dysfunction.

My wife was an hour late to our gym session today.

Left me weighting.

What do you call a broken can opener?

A can't opener.

Made a belt out of wrist watches.

It was a waist of time.

Once saw Prince in concert for £30

Partied like it was £19.99 though.

Anyone need an ark built?

I Noah guy.

Did you know you can hear the blood moving through your veins?

You just have to listen varicosely.

The guy who stole my diary has died.

My thoughts are with his family.

Just bought a first aid kit.

Thought I'd treat myself.

I don't like elevators.

I've been taking steps to avoid them.

I hate the broken bridge in my town.

I just can't get over it.

The guy who invented the POLO made a
mint.

I know a Croatian sound engineer.

And I know a Czech one-two.

What's E.T. short for?

He's only got little legs.

Whoever stole my antidepressants....

I hope you're happy now!

My friend asked if I would stop singing Wonderwall by Oasis.

I said maybe.

My landlord wants to talk with me about why my heating bill is always so high.

I said "sure, my door is always open".

My Uncle died when we couldn't remember his blood type.

As he died he kept saying "be positive", but it's been hard without him around.

I asked my wife if I'm the only one she's been with.

She said "yes, the rest were all 7's and 8's".

Professional hide and seek will never take off.

It's hard to find really good players.

If you rearrange the letters of MAILMEN

They become VERY ANGRY.

What did the Pirate say when he turned 80?

Aye Matey.

I was kidnapped by a mime once.

He did unspeakable things to me.

Australia's biggest export is boomerangs.

It's also their biggest import.

What did the cannibal do after he dumped his girlfriend?

He flushed.

There are two kinds of people in this world.

People who finish their sentences, and

I tried suing an airline for misplacing my
luggage.

I lost my case.

I've never thought of owning a telescope
before.

But it's something I'd look into.

Just found out you can't put cutlery in
toasters.

I was shocked.

The surgeon who operated on my dog was covered in salt and pepper.

He was a seasoned vet.

What do sprinters eat before a race?

They don't – they fast!

My cousin had a flashbulb removed from his bum.

He was delighted.

I saw a sculptor who made artworks out of cuts of steak.

It is a rare medium, but well done.

Bought my wife a prosthetic leg for Christmas.

It's not her main present, just a stocking filler.

What music do wind turbines listen to?

They're big metal fans.

Had a reversing camera installed into my car recently.

Haven't looked back since.

Male bees die after mating.

Call it a honey, nut, cheerio.

My ex dumped me because I wasn't as interesting as I told her I was.

I said I was INTO RESTING.

Bought my wife a castle shaped abacus for her birthday.

It's the fort that counts.

The three unwritten rules of life:
1:
2:
3:

What do you call a factory with average products?

Satisfactory.

What kind of tea do they drink on the set of Grand Designs?

Proper tea.

My personal trainer wanted to find out how flexible I am.

I told him I can't do Thursdays.

What do you call a farmer who doesn't like tractors anymore?

An extractor fan.

I like waiters.

They bring a lot to the table.

Didn't want to believe my brother was stealing from his job as a road worker.

But when I got home, all the signs were there.

My Mum is a radiologist, met my Dad when he came in for an X-Ray.

I wonder what she saw in him.

If your parachute fails to open, don't worry!

You have the rest of your life to figure it out.

"Siri why do I have so much bad luck with women?"

I'm Alexa.

I ate a clock for lunch today.

It was time consuming.

I told my German taxi driver to pull over so I could buy a hot dog.

My journey took a turn for the wurst.

My wife left me for being too insecure.

Hold on, she's back.
She was just making a cup of tea.

Spent 10k on a limousine and it doesn't come
with a driver.

Can't believe I spent all that money and have
nothing to chauffeur it.

Chinese takeaway £15.00
Parking to pick it up £1.00
Getting home to find out they forgot part of
your order?

Riceless.

This is the first year I won't be travelling
because of Covid.

Usually it's because I'm poor.

What has four wheels and flies?

A garbage truck.

I asked this guy if he knew the name of Liverpool's training ground.

"Melwood" he replied.

I said "OK thanks, can you tell me where I can find Mel to ask"?

Did you hear about the blind circumciser?

He got the sack.

What do frogs say when they're horny?

Rubbit.

Reading a book on anti-gravity at the moment.

Can't put it down.

Autocorrect can go straight to he'll.

Did you hear about the monkeys who shared an amazon account?

They're Prime mates

My three favourite things are eating my family and not using commas.

Two guys got caught stealing a calendar.

They got six months each.

I told my doctor "Doc I think I'm addicted to Twitter"

Doctor replied "I'm sorry, I don't follow you?"

Wigs are great.

You've got to take your hat off for them.

Watched a documentary about beavers.

Was the best dam documentary I've ever seen.

Bought a really cheap thesaurus.

Can't find the words to emphasize how bad it is.

A lot of people cry when they cut onions.

The trick is to not get too emotionally attached to them.

Asked my French friend if they like to play games.

She said "Wii"

What kind of ship can't you see?

Censorship.

My girlfriend broke up with me for always referencing computer games.

I thought "that's a strange thing to Fallout 4"

Was dreaming I was swimming in an ocean of orange soda.

Turns out it was just a Fanta sea.

Why do riot police get to work early?

To beat the morning crowds.

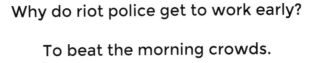

I was hospitalized for eating 12 toy horses recently.

The doctor described my condition as stable.

My ex girlfriend owned a Tazer.

She was a stunner.

English kids are kind but German kids are Kinder.

Who's the nicest guy in the hospital?

The ultrasound guy.

I used to have a job drilling holes for water.

It was well boring.

How do you spot the blind man at the nudist beach?

It's not hard.

My friend told me she doesn't understand human cloning.

I said "that makes two of us".

Accidentally bought glue stick instead of chap stick.

My wife hasn't spoken to me since.

My Grandad had the heart of a lion.

They don't let him in the zoo anymore.

I used to be into investment banking.

But then I lost interest.

I used to make clown shoes for a living.

No small feat.

I lost my mood ring.

Not sure how I feel about it.

It takes guts to make sausages.

I'm addicted to brake fluid.

I can stop at any time though.

Don't invest in funeral companies.

That's a dying industry.

You have a bladder infection?

Unrine trouble.

I used to run an origami business.

The company folded.

Somebody threw a bottle of omega 3 pills at me.

Luckily my injuries are only super fish oil.

Started a new Vegan diet this week.

It's NUTS!

Always tip the pizza chef.

They knead the dough.

Mountains aren't just funny.

They're hill areas.

I used to recycle shoes for a living.

It was sole destroying.

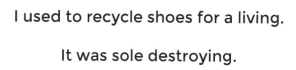

Atheism is a non-prophet organization.

Jokes about COVID.
Contagious aren't they?

Nah, they're just sick jokes.

Person selling me a Christmas tree asked if I
was going to be putting it up myself.

I said "that's disgusting... I'm putting it up in
the living room".

What's the difference between a hippo and a Zippo?

One's really heavy, the other's a little lighter.

Guy threw a lump of cheese at me today.

I thought "That's mature".

If the Pope believes in God..

Why are his windows bulletproof?

RIP Boiling Water....

You will be mist.

How do you milk sheep?

Bring out a new iPhone and charge £1000 for it.

Have you heard about the new corduroy pillows?

They're making headlines!

How do you organize a party in space?

You planet.

Bro, do you want this catalog?

Brochure.

What do you do when you see a spaceman?

Park in it dude.

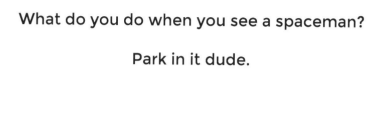

Bought a universal remote the other day and thought..

"This changes everything".

To the person who stole my glasses.... I'll find you!!

I have contacts!

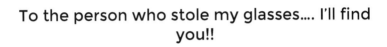

If you're not good at grinding herbs then you're just wasting your thyme.

I watched a documentary on LSD last night.

I think I'm going to start watching all documentaries that way.

How did the mathematician solve his constipation problem?

He worked it out using a pencil.

I sold my vacuum on eBay.

It was just collecting dust.

I went to the zoo the other day and the only animal they had was one dog!

It was a Shih-tzu.

I really look up to my tall friends.

I got addicted to bath salts.

But I'm clean now.

My new girlfriend looks after bees.

My parents think she's a keeper.

My therapist told me to write letters to the people who hurt me and then burn them.

I did that, but now I don't know what to do with all these letters.

I play triangle in a reggae band.

I just stand at the back and ting.

My Dad signed me up for organ donation.

He's a man after my own heart.

I went into the bakers and all the cakes were £1, except for one which was £2.
I asked "what's that cake £2 for?"

They replied "That's Madeira cake".

Watched a documentary on how they kept the panels of the Titanic together.

It was riveting.

I've visited a website which tells me to keep pressing F5 on my keyboard.

It's been refreshing.

I lost my job at the calendar factory.

I only took one day off!

I replaced my double bed with a trampoline today.

My wife hit the roof.

It takes a lot of balls to play golf the way I do.

I have an inferiority complex.

But it's not a very good one.

A man knocked on my door asking for a donation for a new swimming pool.

So I gave him a glass of water.

Worst pub I ever went to was called The Fiddle.

It was a Vile Inn.

People with Dad Bods have a great Father Figure.

A man tried selling me a coffin today.

I thought "That's the last thing I need".

People tell me the back of my head looks really nice.

I can't see it personally.

Adam & Eve were the first people to ignore
Apple's terms and conditions.

A book fell on my head this morning.

I only have my shelf to blame.

Why were people panic buying toilet paper before lockdown?

Assholes.

I ran out of toilet paper and had to start using newspapers instead.

The Times are rough.

My friend has been talking behind my back in the pub, saying I always dodge buying a round.

I'll make him pay for that.

The problem isn't that obesity runs in my family.

The problem is that nobody runs in my family.

You don't need a parachute to go skydiving.

You do need a parachute to go skydiving TWICE.

I don't understand people who want to become archeologists.

Their career is in ruins.

I used to breed rabbits.

Was a hare raising experience.

Siri keeps telling me not to call her Shirley.

I had my phone on airplane mode.

Farting in an elevator is wrong on so many levels.

I'm reading a book about poltergeists.

It's a real page turner.

What do you call a magician who has lost his magic?

Ian.

There was a guy at the supermarket today, he had two trolleys full of Paella and Chorizo.

I thought to myself....
Hispanic buying.

Somebody stole my limbo stick last night.

How low can you go?

Be careful not to get addicted to riding water slides.

It's a slippery slope.

They say the camera adds ten pounds.

I've started taking photos of my wallet, I'll let you know.

Highlighter pens are the future.

Mark my words.

If you don't clean a mirror properly it'll reflect badly on you.

I like making jokes about most types of stationery.

But rulers are where I draw the line.

I used to wear a suit made out of knives.

It was uncomfortable but I looked sharp in it.

I saw a sign that read "Men's Trousers 50% Off"

Turns out they were selling shorts.

It wouldn't be a proper Plastician book of Dad Jokes without some music jokes would it?

Some are a bit niche, but here we go...

I am watching a Netflix series about Berghain.

It's great but it is hard to get into it.

They asked me on Desert Island Discs what is the record I would like to take with me to a desert island.

I said "the record for long distance swimming".

My neighbour rang my door bell at 3am this morning.

Luckily I was still up playing my drums at the time.

What's made of brass and sounds like Tom Jones?

Trombones.

There's no point asking Jammer who his favourite foreign politician is.

We already know he's a Merkel Man.

How does Bob Marley like his birthday cake?

Wi' Jammin.

Rick Astley will lend you almost any of his Disney Pixar DVD's.

But he's never gonna give you Up.

How do you turn a duck into a soul singer?

Put it in the microwave until it's Bill Withers.

Why did General Levy get lost in the Rain Forest?

Jungle Is Massive.

How many Dubstep fans did it take to change a lightbulb?

One to change it, 10 to complain they preferred it when it was darker.

For all my DJ's out there, COVID-19 may have completely ruined 2020, but here's some jokes to help lighten the mood...

What's the difference between the Welsh Football team and DJ's in 2020?

The Welsh Team have got Giggs this year.

What do DJ's and white water rafts have in common?

They only work on live streams.

What do Tories have in common with the Seal Protection Group?

They both hate clubbing.

What do headline DJ's have in common with their bank accounts in 2020?

They both struggle to stay out of the red.

THANK YOU.

KEEP SMILING.

X

Printed in Great Britain
by Amazon